# The Last Gospel

# The Last Gospel

## "...everyone ...shall be saved." Acts 2:21

Mignon R. Spencer

Dante's Publishing • Atlanta, GA

# Foreword

The Haiti catastrophe was the most horrific disaster that I have observed in my lifetime. I cried with the Haitians. I prayed for them. I asked God's mercy upon them. My heart went out to their situation. Every time I saw the body of a child I cried. It felt like it was my child. I knew why I felt their pain and suffering so deeply, because I saw them as an extension of me. I saw them as my brothers and sisters I wanted to help. I wanted to hug them, to give a bottle of water or a box of food.I wanted to help dig someone out from under the rubble. I rejoiced when one of my sisters or brothers was found alive. At first, I didn't understand completely why this catastrophe happened in Haiti and the reason it touched me so deeply. Then I remembered what is written in Matthew 24 in the new testament of the *Holy Bible*.

Jesus spoke of the end of the age and signs for which we should watch. *The Last Gospel: ...everyone ....shall be saved." Acts 2:21* summarizes po-etically what Jesus said to His disciples when he was sitting on the Mount of Olives. According to scripture, they asked him this question: "Tell us... what will be the sign of your coming and the end of the age?" Jesus said, "Watch out that no man deceives you...."

I Thessalonians 5:3 reads: "While people are saying peace and safety, de-struction will come suddenly as labor pains on a pregnant woman and they will not escape. " I believe the day of the Lord is closer than we once thought. No man knows the hour, day or year. Do not be alarmed and fearful but con-tinue to love all, watch and pray through the birth pains... and until He comes.

I dedicate this little book to those Believers who are looking

to that glorious day when The Christ returns.

# The Last Gospel

**Shaloam!**

**Namaste!**

**Assalamu 'Alaikum!**

**Greetings to the Children of God!**

The earth is in labor pains for a New Earth!

It's groaning for the manifestation of God's children.

When the earthquakes come, the earth will shake

Like a quivering womb, her water will break

In great travail, she will begin to push out a new world

She'll scream, she'll cry and she'll ask, "Why us Lord?"

In her anguish, she won't remember what was written.

When the disciples asked Jesus that  sunny day

"What is the sign of the end of the age?"

Jesus indicates that before His future coming

No stone will be left that was laid.

How will the new age be birthed?

Many will come saying "I am the Christ"

You must <u>not</u> believe them

You'll hear of wars, rumors of wars, too!

Keep your calm, don't fear for your life

As such things must happen near you

But the end is still to come.

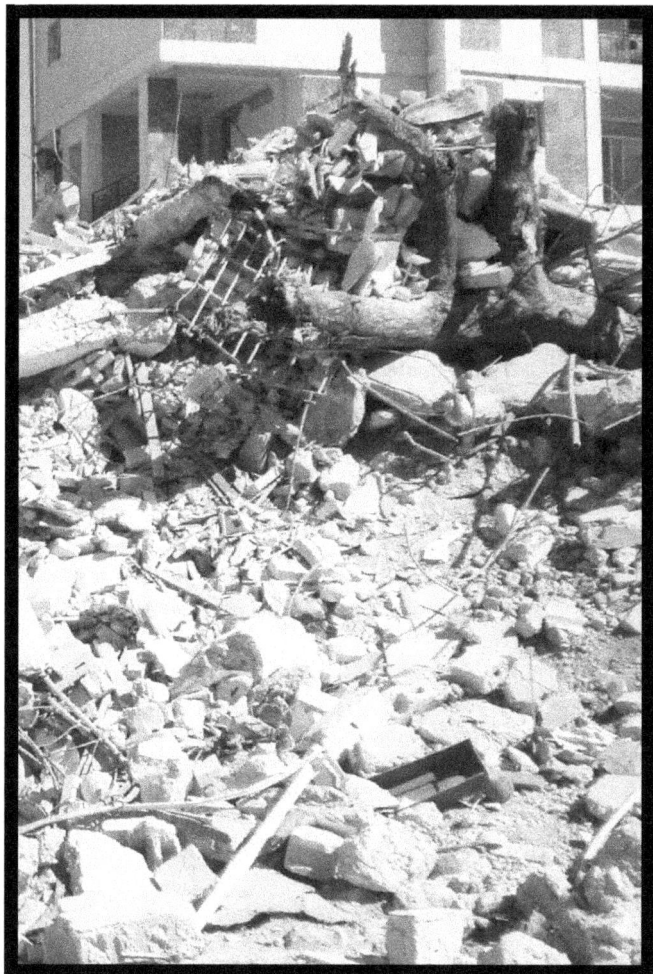

Nation will rise against nation;

Kingdom will be against kingdom;

and famine  will be in various places

Indonesia, Africa, Haiti, China,

Pakistan and many different places.

You'll be persecuted because of Me and

Many false prophets will deceive many people.

People do not love life or each other anymore

Because of increasing wickedness in the world.

This gospel concerning the *End of the Age*

Will be preached throughout the whole world. . .

then the end will come!

Both God's sons and daughters will prophesy.

When the "Abomination that causes Desolation" appears,

Great counterfeit signs and miracles will be performed

To deceive even the elect. . . if that were possible.

"Remember, I have told you ahead of time."

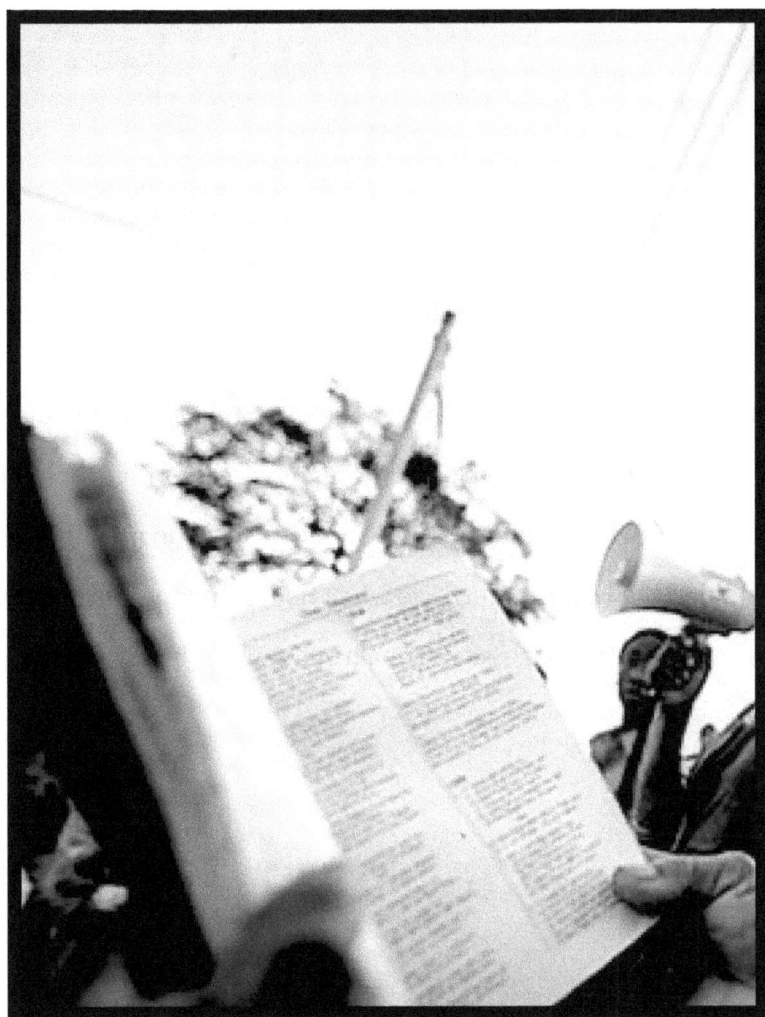

People will flee to the mountain of God-- into relationships with Him.

All people, all religions will join together as children of the Most High.

There will be a terrible time of distress and mourning

Around the world. . .much like when Haiti's labor began in 2009.

The world witnessed her pain and saw her blood flow.

Human carcasses will be piled high in divers places and
Vultures will fly over because of the stench of common burial.
The days will be cut short due to the people of God in the land.
Then, the sun will stop shining: The earth will be cold.
The moon will stop giving its light: The earth will see floods.
Stars will fall from the sky: The earth will be dark.

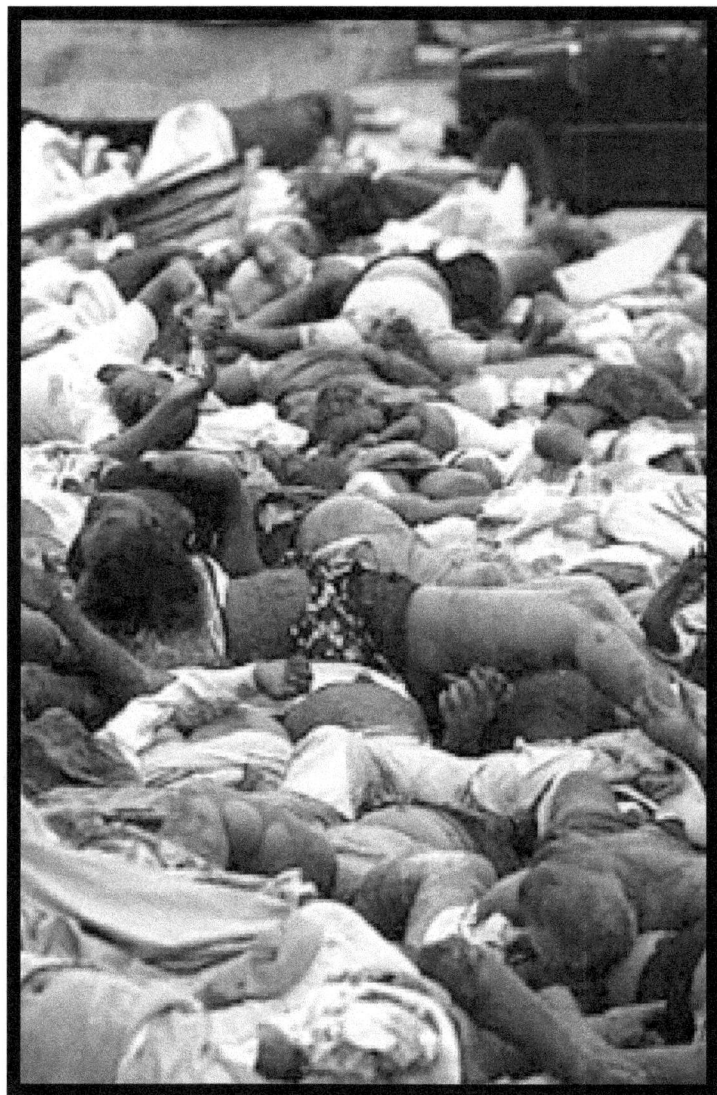

The Galaxies will be shaken: "We will see the crowning."

When you see these things, know that your redemption is near!

Then the sign of the Son of God will appear in the sky.

Everyone will have a panoramic view and in unison began to worship Him.

The people of God will be gathered from the four hemispheres.

There will be a great separation of those who love God and

Those who never really knew the Master or the Son.

They never fed the hungry. They never gave water to the thirsty.

They never visited anyone in prison. They never visited the sick.

They looked the other way when they met a stranger.

They didn't minister love.

Not all of them who said Lord, Lord! will be get on board.

The old earth we once knew, will no longer exist.

Whomsoever shall call upon the only Living God will be saved!

And a new heaven and new earth will come forth!

Encourage those that you meet with these words.

# The Bride of Christ

Love the Lord with all your heart and soul

And love your neighbor as you have been told.


The King of Glory shall come! Watch, read and pray

For the Father is sending back The Son one day.


Greet Mr. Jones when you meet him at the mail box

That child without a Dad just needs some new socks


Her husband died last week; help her with her flowerbeds

That young man went home and found his best friend dead.


Live the message of love in your own neighborhood

That elderly man needs some help with chopping wood


A grandson is in prison; wont you visit him next week?

Notice that bag lady who has had nothing to drink or eat


The flood waters washed their brand new home away

A donation would find a place for their heads to lay

The Word declares that disasters are surely to come along

Comfort will be found in knowing to whom you belong


Whether  Jewish, Muslim, Hindu, Buddhist,

gay, straight, black or white

God loves you all. You are precious in His sight.


The King of Glory shall come! Watch, read and pray

For the Father is sending back The Son one day.


Love the Lord with all your heart and soul

And love your neighbor as you have been told.

World Religions are looking for the coming of the following:

Maitreya ( (Future Buddha)

The Christ (The Christian's Annointed One)

Kalki (The Hindu's Destroyer of Darkness)

Saoshyant (The Zoastrian's One Who Brings Benefit)

The Mahdi (Islam's Guided One)

Until He comes...may the God of heaven be with you.

# ABOUT THE AUTHOR

✺

Poet, writer, and teacher **Mignon Spencer** was born and raised outside Atlanta, Georgia, where she has lived most of her adult life. Mignon is the author of two poetry collections *Pearls from the Soul, The Maze,* and her children's book *I'm Living My Dream.* She is also the founder of Ever Increasing Kingdom Ministries, whose mission is to remind God's children to prepare for end-time events. She and her husband reside in Hampton, Georgia.

Published in the United States by Dante's Publishing, LLC

www.dantespublishing.com

ISBN: 978-0-9827949-0-6

Scriptural references used in this writing are taken from the *New International Version* of the Bible, Copyright 1984.

Thanks to Gaynell Harbin for sharing photos from Haiti.

Cover Design by Taneka Badie

# Notes

# Notes

# Notes

www.ingramcontent.com/pod-product-compliance
Lightning Source LLC
Chambersburg PA
CBHW060559030426

42337CB00019B/3572